Mindful Mantras

I Can Handle Special Occasions!

By Laurie Wright

My name is Sebastien,
and I can handle special occasions!

I am so **impatient** when I have to wait for a special day!
Can I handle it?

I can try to keep busy.

I can pass the time playing with my little sister.

I can help my mom with her to-do list.

I can handle waiting!

I get worried when it's time for summer holidays.
I can handle it though.

I can keep in touch with my school friends.

I can have fun with my family.

I can sleep in every morning.

I can handle summer holidays!

I get **nervous** when there are events with loud noises. Can I handle it?

I can wear my special loud noise protection suit.

I can stick with my best friend so I feel safe.

I can wear earmuffs so the loud noise doesn't bother me.

I can handle loud noises!

I feel **overwhelmed** when there is a celebration and lots of people come for dinner.
How do I handle it?

I can go to my room when I need a break.

I can tell my mom how I feel so she'll help me.

I can take deep breaths to calm down.

I can handle celebrations with lots of people!

I feel jealous when my sister gets presents.
I'm not sure how to handle that.

I can try to be happy for her.

I can remember when it will be my turn to get presents.

I can ask to help her open her presents.

I can handle presents!

I feel **stressed** out when I have to eat food I'm not used to at someone else's house!
How do I handle it?

I can start with the food I'm used to.

I can ask for some ketchup.

I can try a little of everything, just to see if I like it.

I can handle new food!

I feel concerned that I won't have enough money to buy presents for my family at holiday time.
How do I handle that?

I can ask to do some chores to earn money.

I can shop at the dollar store.

I can make presents instead of buying them.

I can handle buying presents.

I feel anxious when it's a holiday and I will miss my teacher.
Can I handle it?

I can draw a picture of her and look at it sometimes.

I can distract myself by playing fun games.

I can count the days until I see her again, so it doesn't seem so long.

I can handle missing my teacher!

I feel **scared** when I see people dressed up in scary costumes.
Can I handle it though?

I can make sure to stay close to an adult.

I can wear X-ray goggles so I know who is wearing the costumes.

I can wear my bravest costume so I know I'll be safe.

I can handle costumes!

I feel lonely when my parents are distracted during busy holiday times.
I think I can handle it.

I can stand close to mom or dad until they aren't busy.

I can wait patiently until they aren't so busy.

I can tell them how I feel and get a hug.

I can handle it when my parents are distracted.

I feel tired when I've stayed up too late at a party. Can I handle it?

I can have a nap, even though I'm too old for naps.

I can try to do quiet things alone.

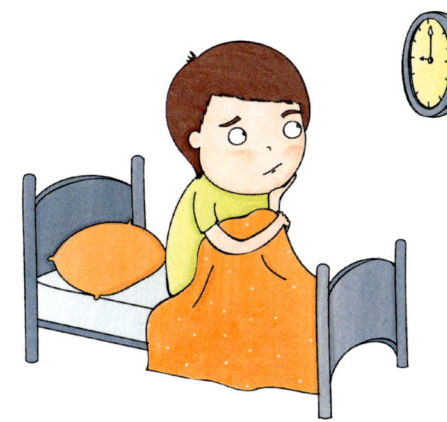

I can go to bed early to catch up on sleep.

I can handle being tired.

I'm sad when people I love are gone or far away.
How will I handle it?

I can share how I feel with people close to me.

I can write a letter to the person I am missing.

I can do something meaningful to keep them in my thoughts.

I can handle missing loved ones.

I'm all **mixed up** when my routine is different during a holiday.
Can I handle it?

I can walk backward to see things in a different way.

I can go for walk to enjoy the sunshine and the outdoors, to help me feel calm.

I can know for sure that my routine will get back to normal soon!

I can handle a different routine.

Sometimes during special occasions I feel impatient, worried, nervous, overwhelmed, tired, scared, lonely, anxious, stressed out, jealous, concerned or sad.

But I can handle it, I can handle special occasions!

My name is

_____

and I can handle special occasions!

Laurie Wright

Laurie Wright is a speaker, author, and educator who is passionate about helping children increase their positive self-talk and improve their mental health. Laurie speaks to parents, teachers, has given a TEDx talk, created resources and has written 3 books, all to further the cause of improving the self-esteem of our children. Laurie is a huge advocate for children's mental health and works every day to improve the way we interact with kids, and to help them learn to handle all of their emotions!

Ana Santos

Ana is a creative and innate illustrator and she feels very comfortable and inspired by all the challenges and areas that incorporate illustration and design. Graduated in graphic design, she dicovered her vocation for Arts as a child. Ana has already several years of experience in graphic design and illustration and she has already illustrated several edited children's books for people and publishers around the world! Ana is an artist attentive to new technologies working on many internet platforms as a freelancer.

Made in the USA
Middletown, DE
28 September 2018